CHESTER TO RHYL

Including the Holywell Town and Dyserth Branches

Vic Mitchell and Keith Smith

MP *Middleton Press*

Front cover: Framed by the curious roofing on the up side at Chester on 30th June 1991 is 4-6-0 no. 46229 Duchess of Hamilton *with the return "North Wales Coast Excursion". British Railways logo and Mk 1 coaches are evident. (T.Heavyside)*

Back cover upper: No. 31439 is passing Point of Ayr Colliery, near Talacre, with the 15.12 Manchester Victoria to Llandudno on 6th August 1994. (H.Ballantyne)

Back cover lower: No. 37408 Loch Rannoch *leaves Rhyl with the 11.58 Birmingham to Holyhead on 7th May 1999. Arrival would be at 15.26, the operator being North Western Trains. (P.Jones)*

Published March 2011

ISBN 978 1 906008 93 2

© Middleton Press, 2011

Design Deborah Esher

Published by
> *Middleton Press*
> *Easebourne Lane*
> *Midhurst*
> *West Sussex*
> *GU29 9AZ*

Tel: 01730 813169
Fax: 01730 812601
Email: info@middletonpress.co.uk
www.middletonpress.co.uk

Printed in the United Kingdom by Henry Ling Limited, at the Dorset Press, Dorchester, DT1 1HD

CONTENTS

INDEX

ACKNOWLEDGEMENTS

We are very grateful for the assistance received from many of those mentioned in the credits also to P.G.Barnes, B.W.L.Brooksbank, A.R.Carder, G.Croughton, M.Dart, S.C.Jenkins, N.Langridge, B.Lewis, J.H.Meredith, Mr D. and Dr S.Salter and in particular, our always supportive wives, Barbara Mitchell and Janet Smith.

I. Railway Clearing House map for the late 1920s, excludes the halts.

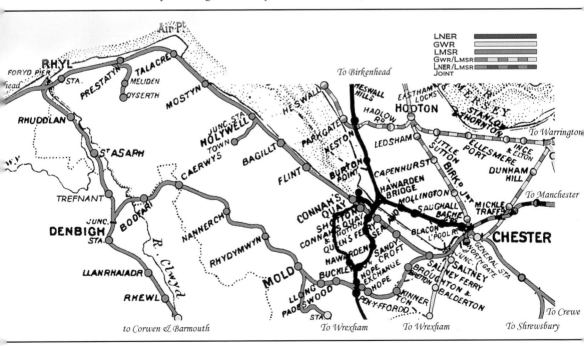

GEOGRAPHICAL SETTING

The route is never far from water: the River Dee from Chester to Talacre and the Irish Sea thereafter. It is thus almost level and has many miles of flood protection measures on its north side. The two branches climb steeply away from it into the northern end of the Clwyd Range. From east to west, this comprises of parallel strips of coal measures, limestone and sandstone, all terminating close to the main line. Chester itself is on sandstone and pebble beds.

The entire route was constructed in Flintshire, except the eastern two miles, which are in Cheshire, the county town of which is Chester, an important commercial and administrative centre since Roman times. Thus all the route, except for two miles, is in Wales.

The maps are to the scale of 25ins to 1 mile, with north at the top unless otherwise indicated. Welsh spelling and hyphenation has varied over the years and so we have generally used the form of the period.

II. Both branches are seen on the 1946 edition at 2ins to 1 mile.
The stations have open circles, but only the Holywell ones were in use by that time.

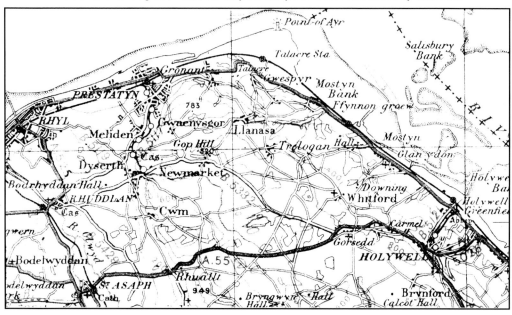

Gradient profile with mileage from Euston.

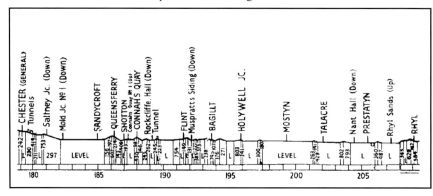

HISTORICAL BACKGROUND

Railways reached Chester from Crewe and from Birkenhead in 1840 and Wrexham in 1846. The latter ran to Shrewsbury in 1848.

The Chester & Holyhead Railway opened from Chester to Bangor on 1st May 1848, the trains of the Shrewsbury & Chester Railway running over it north of Saltney Junction from 4th November 1846. (The latter company became part of the Great Western Railway in 1854.) The C&HR Act was passed on 4th July 1844 and its engineer was Robert Stephenson.

The route was acquired by the London & North Western Railway on 18th March 1859, the company having operated all the trains since its opening.

Chester received the Birkenhead, Lancashire & Cheshire Junction Railway in 1850, the Cheshire Lines Committee trains from the east in 1874 and from the west came the Manchester, Sheffield & Lincolnshire Railway in 1890.

The LNWR became a constituent of the London Midland & Scottish Railway in 1923 and its area formed the London Midland Region of British Railways upon nationalisation in 1948.

Privatisation brought trains of Wales & West on 13th October 1996. The name was Wales & Borders from 6th November 2001 and Arriva Trains Wales from 7th December 2003. Long distance services were worked by Virgin Trains from 9th March 1997. North Western Trains operated trains from Lancashire from 2nd March 1997 until 2004, when ATW took over.

Holywell Branch

This was built on the route of the Holywell Railway, a mineral line in use from 1860 for almost 20 years. The branch was opened by the LNWR on 1st July 1912 for goods and passengers. It closed to all traffic on 6th September 1954, except for a short length to a private siding.

Dyserth Branch

Constructed under an Act of 16th July 1866, this steeply graded line came into use for mineral traffic on 1st September 1869. A passenger service was provided from Prestatyn from 28th August 1905 until 22nd September 1930, but a reversal outside that station was necessary on every journey. Mineral trains continued on most of the length of the branch until 7th September 1973.

July 1924

February 1936

PASSENGER SERVICES

	Weekdays	Sundays
1849	5	3
1859	8	4
1869	13	5
1889	15	5
1924	16	5
1939	48	12
1958	41	5
1985	25	13
2011	29	19

The initial timetable showed four trains on weekdays, with two on Sundays. Four months after opening, this was increased to six and three. Subsequent sample Summer services are shown left.

Not included are the one or two short workings that ran in the late steam era. There were many extras on Summer Saturdays, notably in the 1930s and the 1950s.

Holywell Town Branch

	Weekdays	Sundays
1912	16	0
1924	21	0
1938	26	17
1948	16	0

Dyserth Branch

No Sunday services were recorded.

1905	8
1911	16
1922	12
1930	16

The Summer timetables in the first few years were increased, as were train lengths (to two coaches) on account of seasonal visitors.

June 1869

CREWE, CHESTER, HOLYWELL, RHYL, LLANDUDNO, LLANRWST, BETTWS-Y-COED, CONWAY, BANGOR, CARNARVON, HOLYHEAD, KINGSTOWN, and DUBLIN.—Chester and Holyhead—L. & N. W.

1. Chester to Rhyl

CHESTER

III. This diagram is based on the 1903 Railway Clearing House issue,
with signal box numbers added.

	Opened	Closed	No. of Levers
No. 1	01.1958	16.09.1973	60
No. 2	12.1890	06.05.1984	182
No. 3	07.1890	07.12.1980	45
No. 3A	09.1962	05.05.1984	85
No. 4	06.1904	06.05.1984	176
No. 5	05.1874	04.05.1984	81
No. 6	07.1903	05.05.1984	80

1. This view of the southeast elevation probably dates from the 1920s, when the amount of glass was diminishing. Most had gone by 1950, as had much of the steel work. Gas for the lights was provided by a local company, but the GWR had made its own for coach lighting. (M.J.Stretton coll.)

IV.   Map III helps to identify the ownership of the tracks, stations and depots shown on this extract from the 1911 edition, scaled at 18ins to 1 mile. General was a joint station from the outset, but there was only one through platform initially, however there were an amazing 36 carriage turntables, soon after. The street tramway terminates below General Station and its depot is nearby. It ran to Saltney and is shown in detail in *Chester Tramways* (Middleton Press).

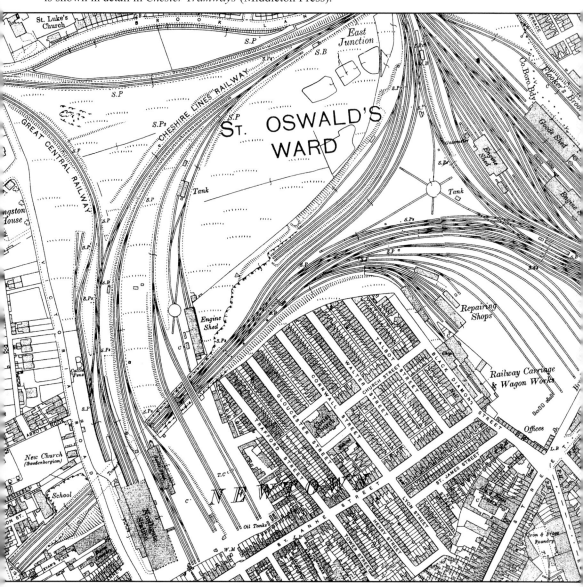

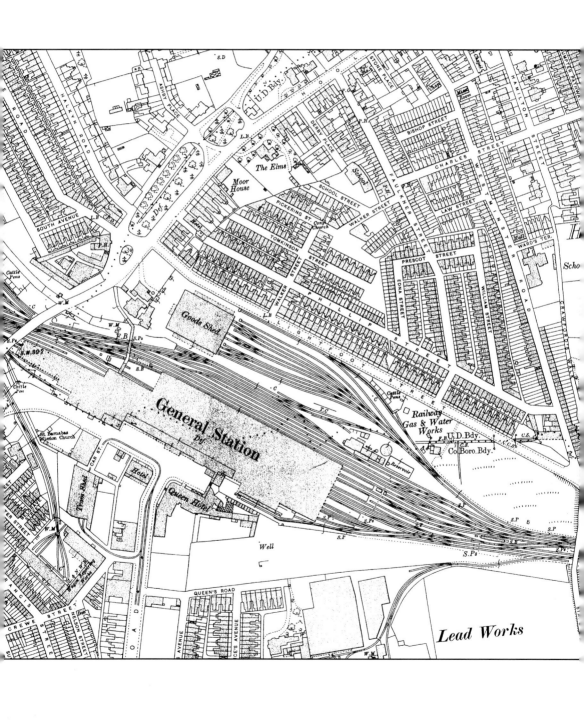

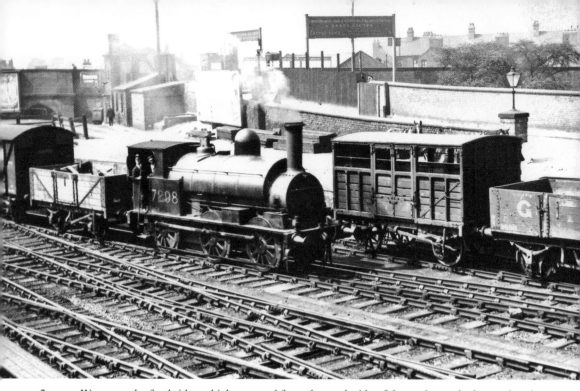

2.	We are on the footbridge which emerged from the north side of the station and witness shunting on 2nd June 1932. The locomotive is an ex-LNWR 0-6-0ST, no. 7208. (H.C.Casserley)

3.	A fine eastward panorama from 10th July 1948 has the station beyond the road bridge and the former GWR engine shed on the left. It had just become BR 84K and was recoded 6E in February 1958. On the right is No. 4 Box. (R.G.Nelson/T.Walsh coll.)

4.   The end of the engine shed is just visible above the leading coach in this view in the opposite direction in about 1953. Hauling the up "Irish Mail" is no. 46149 *The Middlesex Regiment*, a 4-6-0 of the "Royal Scot" class. (A.W.V.Mace/Milepost 92½)

5.   The town frontage was photographed in 1958. This was the original building and it is well conserved today. The suffix "General" was used from time to time, but was discontinued on 6th May 1970, following the closure of other Chester stations. (H.C.Casserley)

6.　　　Passing No. 4 Box with petrol tankers is a class 4F 0-6-0, sometime in the mid-1950s. The ex-GWR engine shed closed in May 1960. (A.W.V.Mace/Milepost 92½)

7.   A view in the same direction from 29th April 1984 shows the new maintenance shed and part of the old engine shed. A tour train is arriving from Shrewsbury behind ex-Southern Region 4-6-2 no. 35028 *Clan Line*. (T.Heavyside)

8.   Another special was recorded on 30th June 1991, this running from Crewe to Holyhead behind 4-6-2 no. 46229 *Duchess of Hamilton*. Unchanged in the background is the Queen Hotel, but the station roofing had altered greatly at the west end. (T.Heavyside)

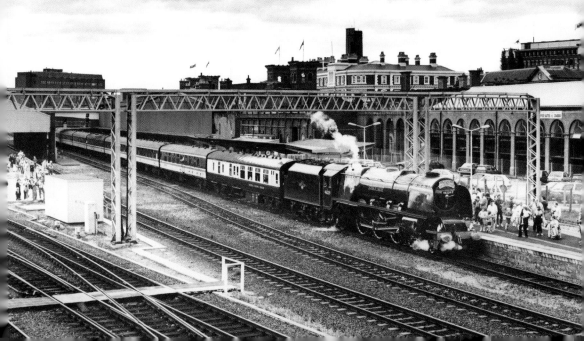

9.   Most of the original brickwork and much of the central structure remained. This is the 15.57 from Liverpool Lime Street on 23rd April 1996. The conductor rail below it was in use from 1992 for trains from Liverpool via Birkenhead. (M.J.Stretton)

Other views of this station and the route to Saltney can be found in our *Shrewsbury to Chester* album in pictures 105-120.

L. M. & S. R.
Issued subject to the conditions&regulations in the Coo Time Tables Books Bills& Notices.

CHESTER   TO

QUEENSFERRY
(E 9)

THIRD
CLASS   37R(E)(S)   FARE -/10
            QUEENSFERRY

1266

10.   We now have two photographs from 7th September 2008. Having obtained your ticket and passed through the barriers (left), the options are the historic staircase or the more recent lifts; a shaft is centre. (V.Mitchell)

11.   On the same level as the barriers is platform 3 and waiting to leave it is the 11.28 Euston to Llandudno, worked by no. 175008. This innovative Virgin Trains service operated only from September 2004 to December 2008. (V.Mitchell)

WEST OF CHESTER

12.   Passing under No. 6 Box on 5th June 1982 is the 09.00 York to Llandudno, hauled by no. 40184. The location is at the centre of the left page of map IV. (T.Heavyside)

13.   It is the same day and no. 47564 is approaching Chester with the 11.57 Bangor to Manchester. The former GWR tracks are on the left. Northgate Street Tunnels are 218yds long and the train is about to enter the 104yd Windmill Lane Tunnel, which has one arch, instead of two. The cutting is only 132yds long. (T.Heavyside)

14.   The west end of Northgate Street Tunnels are seen in the 1930s as an LMS train emerges from the No. 2 bore. Resignalling of the area began in 1978 and the two tracks on the right were both designated "Down", subsequently. (R.S.Carpenter coll.)

SOUTH OF CHESTER

15.   The 15.40 Manchester to Bangor is curving south as it crosses the Shropshire Union Canal, the locks of which are on the right. The date is 7th July 1973 and the train will soon pass Chester Racecourse, which is on the right of picture 17. (T.Heavyside)

16.   The first bridge was designed by Robert Stephenson and comprised cast iron girders on two stone piers. One section collapsed when the 6.15pm to Ruabon was passing over it on 24th May 1847. There were four deaths. The bridge was rebuilt with wrought iron in 1871. (Illustrated London News)

17.   Crossing the River Dee sometime in the 1950s is 0-6-0PT no. 8730 with empty wagons for Gresford Colliery. The two spans on the left deteriorated and traffic was concentrated on the other two from 1979. The convergence of the tracks from four to two takes place at the far end of the 49-arch Roodee Viaduct. The spans on the right were completed by the GWR in 1904 and allowed the quadrupling between Chester and Saltney Junction. A 15-lever block post was provided in 1907 at Crane Street, it closing on 16th April 1967. (Milepost 92½)

SALTNEY JUNCTION

18.		The 60-lever 1902 signal box is in the background and was just beyond the right border of the map. This train has taken the curve from the south and is hauled by ex-GWR 4-6-0 no. 7812 *Erlestoke Manor* probably in the 1950s. The box closed on 25th February 1973, but the locomotive was preserved. (Bentley coll.)

V.		Our route is across this 1913 map at 7ins to 1 mile and the GWR's main line curves south. Its station, sidings and wharf are illustrated in our *Shrewsbury to Chester* album. The tramway terminus was in Chester Street. The dots and dashes mark the county and national boundary.

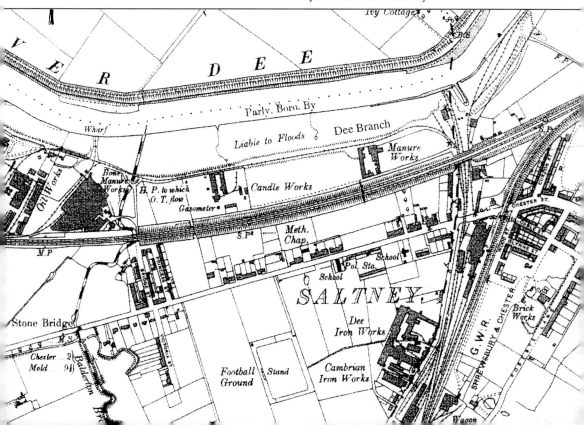

SALTNEY FERRY

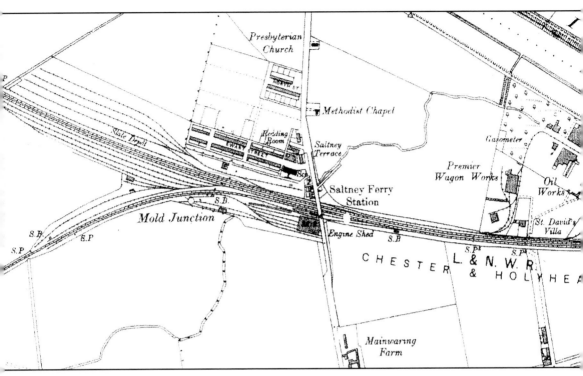

VI.   This is a continuation of the previous map and reveals that the private sidings from the GWR and the LNWR link up in the industrial complex. All the dwellings were for LNWR staff.

19.   The single island platform (right) opened on 1st January 1891 and the quadrupling followed in July 1899. The engine shed was completed in 1890 and is on the right. The bridge replaced a level crossing for Saltney Lane in 1874. The turntable was changed from 42ft to 60ft in 1934. (Postcard)

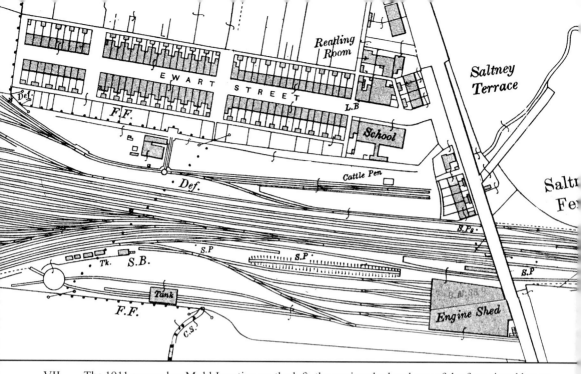

VII.   The 1911 survey has Mold Junction on the left, the engine shed and one of the four signal boxes having that name. No. 2 Box is on the left, along with the 1849 line curving south to Mold. The upper sidings on the left served slate sorting wharves and could take 393 wagons.

20.   We have a view west from No. 2 Box in the 1930s, with the Mold branch in the left foreground and the main line signals in the background, together with No. 4 Box. This was of timber construction and was built in 1896 with 35 levers. It was replaced by one with a flat concrete roof and 55 levers in 1945. This would be resistant to incendiary bombs. The 1890 marshalling yard on the left could take 900 wagons. Slate wharves can be seen on the right. They all closed in October 1979. (British Railways)

21.   The west end of the engine shed is seen in the 1950s, along with the end of the platform. The BR shed code was 6B and the allocation was 44 locomotives in 1959 and 28 in 1965. (R.S.Carpenter)

22.   Looking east on 6th October 1964, we see the platform, which was closed on 30th April 1962. In the distance is No. 1 Box and on the right is the north wall of the engine shed. (R.J.Essery/R.S.Carpenter)

23.   Seen on the same day is the unimposing passenger entrance. The name was derived from the nearby salt marshes. The ferry ran until a footbridge was built in the 1960s. (R.J.Essery/R.S.Carpenter)

24.   Over the pit on 18th February 1966 is 4-6-0 class 5 no. 44778 and to the right of the coaling plant is No. 2 Box. The 1877 structure contained 30 levers and was in use until 18th August 1968. No. 4 closed on 26th February 1978, leaving only No.1. No.3 was on the branch. On the left is the ash plant, which raised tubs from the ground and tipped them into the wagons on the left. (T.Heavyside)

25.   On the right was Mold Junction goods yard, which had a cattle dock. Freight traffic continued until 4th May 1964. The deserted island platform was recorded in 1966, the year in which the engine shed (left) was closed. The turntable is now preserved at Rowsley South on Peak Rail. (Stations UK)

26.   We look east from the bridge on 8th August 1982 at No. 1 Box, Hawarden Airfield and the 09.34 Stoke on Trent to Llandudno. There were two down lines in use, but only one up, by that time. (D.H.Mitchell)

27.　　Rushing across the road, we see the same train passing the site of the platform, which had been between the tracks on the left. Compare this picture with no. 25 and gasp! The line on the left served a spoil tip in the slate yard, but reversal was necessary. Dobbins had a scrap metal yard on the locomotive depot site until July 1983. (D.H.Mitchell)

28.　　No. 1 Box had 60 levers when opened in November 1902 and was staffed until 24th January 2005. It housed electronic equipment from 1984. There were emergency signals for use if there were problems with aircraft flying too low at Hawarden Airfield. The HST is working the 08.53 Euston to Holyhead on 11th October 1991. (T.Heavyside)

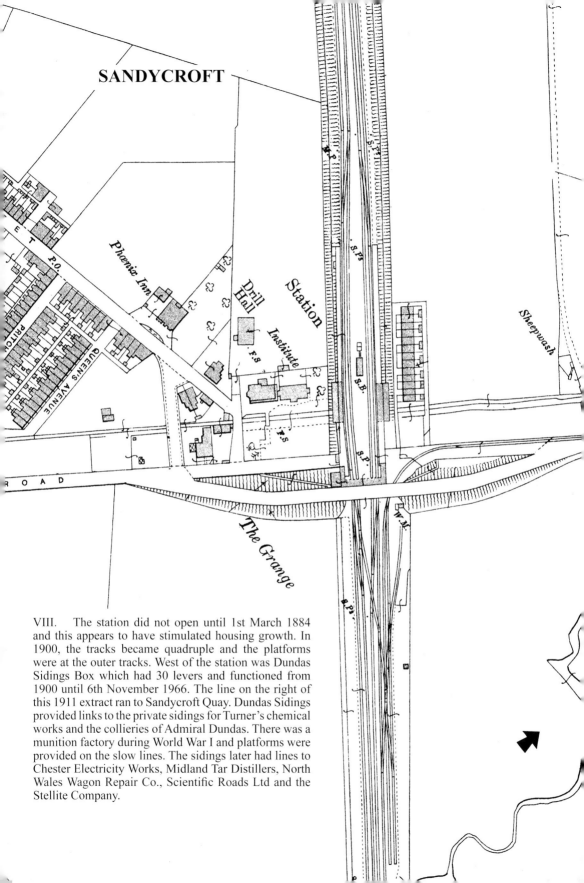

SANDYCROFT

Phoenix Inn

Drill Hall

Station

Institute

Sheepwash

Queen's Avenue

Prince *ROAD*

P.O.

The Grange

VIII.   The station did not open until 1st March 1884 and this appears to have stimulated housing growth. In 1900, the tracks became quadruple and the platforms were at the outer tracks. West of the station was Dundas Sidings Box which had 30 levers and functioned from 1900 until 6th November 1966. The line on the right of this 1911 extract ran to Sandycroft Quay. Dundas Sidings provided links to the private sidings for Turner's chemical works and the collieries of Admiral Dundas. There was a munition factory during World War I and platforms were provided on the slow lines. The sidings later had lines to Chester Electricity Works, Midland Tar Distillers, North Wales Wagon Repair Co., Scientific Roads Ltd and the Stellite Company.

29.   An up train approaches the 1900 building; there are staff cottages on the right. By 1938, there were private sidings for N.H.Graesser and the International Electrolytic Plant Company. (Lens of Sutton coll.)

30.   Closure to goods and passenger traffic took place on 1st May 1961. The 10.30 Manchester Victoria to Llandudno is about to pass under the bridge on 8th August 1982, as we gain a glimpse of the former goods dock. (D.H.Mitchell)

31. The signal box had 60 levers and was built in 1900. It was in use until 24th January 2005. Speeding through on 14th August 1993 is no. 37408 *Loch Rannoch* with the 12.06 Llandudno to Birmingham New Street. Track simplification took place in 1986. (H.Ballantyne)

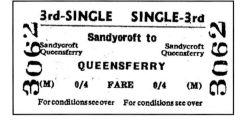

QUEENSFERRY

IX.   The station opened with the line as Queens Ferry and was rebuilt in 1900 during the quadrupling. As at Sandycroft, provision was made for an island platform, which never materialised. The booking office is near the D of STATION ROAD, adjacent to the gateway to the goods yard. A 5-ton crane was added later.

32. Standard LNWR buildings replaced the original ones and are seen in about 1923. The house for the station master faced the drive to the goods yard, in the interests of security. (Stations UK)

33. The goods shed (left) was built in 1870 and freight traffic continued until 14th May 1964. The platforms and their buildings were supported on wooden trestles. (Lens of Sutton coll.)

34. The signal box had a 60-lever frame and functioned from July 1900 until 6th November 1966. Passenger service was withdrawn on 19th February 1966. (Lens of Sutton coll.)

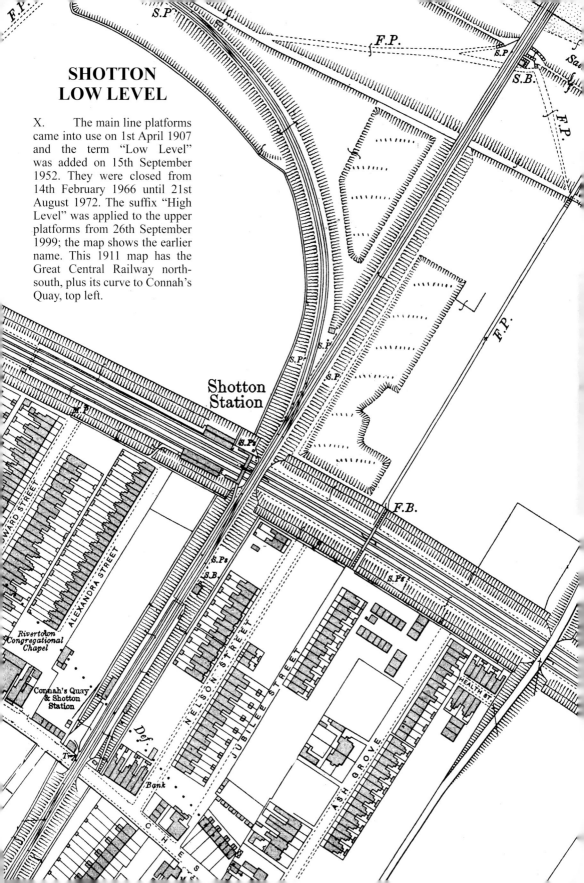

SHOTTON
LOW LEVEL

X.   The main line platforms
came into use on 1st April 1907
and the term "Low Level"
was added on 15th September
1952. They were closed from
14th February 1966 until 21st
August 1972. The suffix "High
Level" was applied to the upper
platforms from 26th September
1999; the map shows the earlier
name. This 1911 map has the
Great Central Railway north-
south, plus its curve to Connah's
Quay, top left.

Shotton
Station

Rivertown
Congregational
Chapel

Connah's Quay
& Shotton
Station

Bank

35.   An eastward view from about 1923 features the passenger footbridge, but it obscures the GCR bridge. By 1907, no attempt had been made to make provision for an island platform here. (Stations UK)

36.   New platforms had to be built for the reopening, but the originals remained in the undergrowth. No. 37429 is passing with the 13.30 Holyhead to Manchester Victoria on 14th August 1993. (H.Ballantyne)

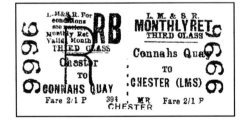

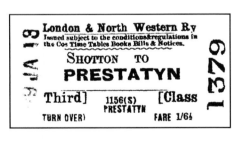

37. The new platforms and the tiny shelter on the up side are evident as a Regional Railways' DMU works the 11.33 Wrexham Central to Bidston service on 24th April 1996. (M.J.Stretton)

38. No. 158783 speeds under the new footbridge on 4th May 1999, as it runs from Bangor to Manchester. "Low Level" had not been reapplied. (P.Jones)

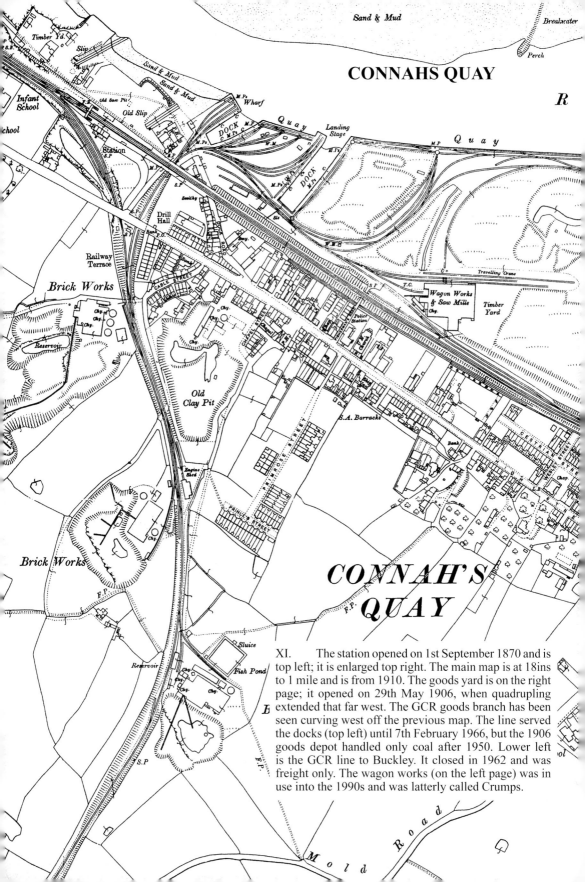

CONNAHS QUAY

R

CONNAH'S
QUAY

XI.   The station opened on 1st September 1870 and is
top left; it is enlarged top right. The main map is at 18ins
to 1 mile and is from 1910. The goods yard is on the right
page; it opened on 29th May 1906, when quadrupling
extended that far west. The GCR goods branch has been
seen curving west off the previous map. The line served
the docks (top left) until 7th February 1966, but the 1906
goods depot handled only coal after 1950. Lower left
is the GCR line to Buckley. It closed in 1962 and was
freight only. The wagon works (on the left page) was in
use into the 1990s and was latterly called Crumps.

39.   Although late on the scene, the architectural style was similar to that employed initially. We look east from the footbridge at the small parcels shed. (Lens of Sutton coll.)

40.   An eastbound freight train largely obscures No. 2 Box in this view from the 1930s. The 15-lever frame was in use from 1870 until 20th December 1953. No. 1 Box was near Wepre Gutter and was open from 1905 until 13th August 1980, when it was destroyed by fire. The frame had 36 levers. (Stations UK)

41.　　The industrial environs are evident as we glimpse at the up platform on 10th August 1953. The LMS retained the apostrophe on their "Hawks Eye" nameboard. (R.M.Casserley)

42.　　A simpler BR "Totem" sign is on the left, as we look west and marvel that the station is gas lit, but in the shadow of a power station. This would soon use gas instead of coal and the station would close to passengers on 14th February 1966. (Lens of Sutton coll.)

43.   BR lost the coal traffic and the generators lost their chimneys not long after no. 47378 was recorded on 8th August 1982, with a Euston to Holyhead train. The gas comes from a plant at Point of Ayr. (D.H.Mitchell)

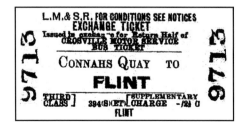

L.M.& S.R. FOR CONDITIONS SEE NOTICES
EXCHANGE TICKET
Issued in exchange for Return Half of
CROSVILLE MOTOR SERVICE
BUS TICKET
CONNAHS QUAY   TO
FLINT
THIRD   SUPPLEMENTARY
CLASS] 394(S)(ET) CHARGE -/2½ 0
FLINT

9713   9713

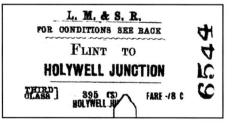

L. M. & S. R.
FOR CONDITIONS SEE BACK
FLINT   TO
HOLYWELL JUNCTION
THIRD   395 (S)   FARE -/8 C
CLASS]   HOLYWELL JU

6544

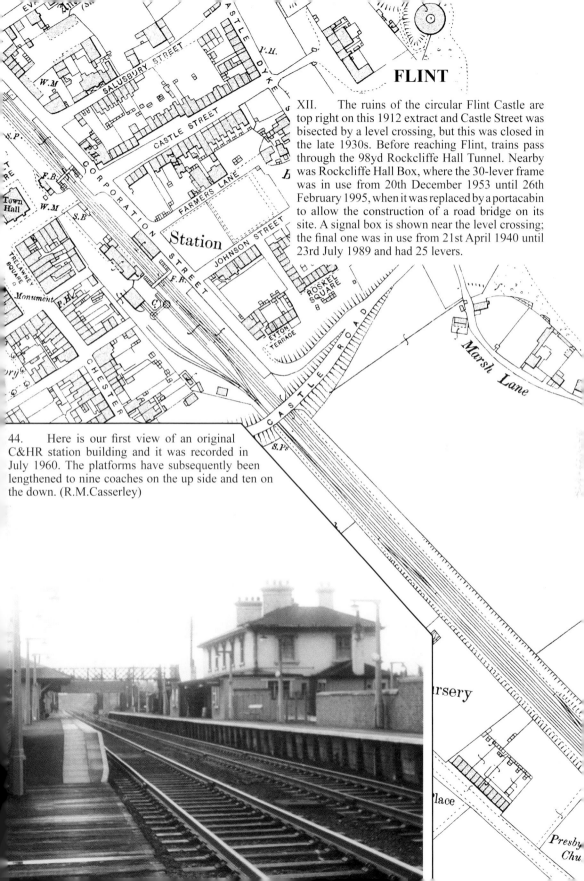

FLINT

XII.   The ruins of the circular Flint Castle are top right on this 1912 extract and Castle Street was bisected by a level crossing, but this was closed in the late 1930s. Before reaching Flint, trains pass through the 98yd Rockcliffe Hall Tunnel. Nearby was Rockcliffe Hall Box, where the 30-lever frame was in use from 20th December 1953 until 26th February 1995, when it was replaced by a portacabin to allow the construction of a road bridge on its site. A signal box is shown near the level crossing; the final one was in use from 21st April 1940 until 23rd July 1989 and had 25 levers.

44.   Here is our first view of an original C&HR station building and it was recorded in July 1960. The platforms have subsequently been lengthened to nine coaches on the up side and ten on the down. (R.M.Casserley)

45.   The goods shed (right) was completed in 1860 and we look from the west on 21st June 1966 at the main building. The population rose from 4279 in 1901 to 13,950 in 1961. (H.C.Casserley)

46.   The building on the up platform was erected in 1883 and was photographed in June 1966. Water troughs were provided southeast of the station in 1895. (H.C.Casserley)

47.　　There were three footbridges in close proximity: the photographer is on one, the other public one is in the distance and the one over the train was restricted to ticket holders. No. 31408 is heading the 13.30 Holyhead to Manchester on 17th July 1993. The goods yard closed on 4th May 1964, but its shed still stands. Both it and the main building are listed structures. (T.Heavyside)

48.　　English Electric Type 3 no. 37422 in Regional Railways colours runs through Flint with the 14.23 Birmingham to Holyhead on 15th May 1999. The train will have just been close to the one mile-long Pentre Sea Wall. There was a 20-lever signal box near it from 1895 to 1967. The Welsh name of Y Fflint has appeared on subsequent signs, but not timetables. (P.Jones)

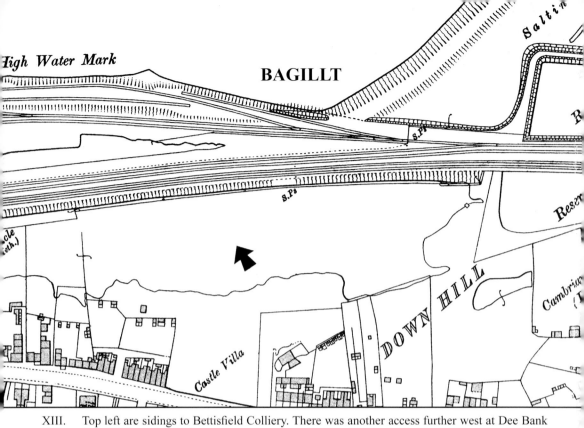

XIII.   Top left are sidings to Bettisfield Colliery. There was another access further west at Dee Bank Sidings Box (40-levers), which was open from June 1907 until July 1951. The 1912 survey includes a further length of quadruple track. The 1938 siding listing included private sidings for H.W.Stothard and two for Courtauld's Greenfield site. Muspratts Siding Box was to the east from 1895 to 1965 and quadrupling was in the 1900s.

49.   A view west from about 1960 features the 1907 72-lever signal box. The Courtaulds siding two miles west was closed in 1985. Lead from local mines had once been smelted here, but the industry had declined by 1900. (Lens of Sutton coll.)

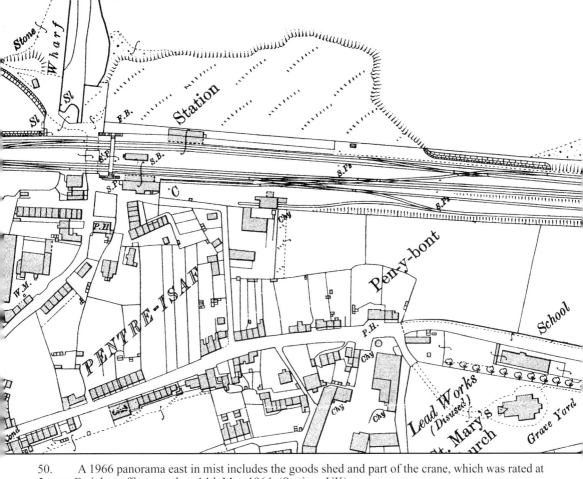

50.   A 1966 panorama east in mist includes the goods shed and part of the crane, which was rated at 5-tons. Freight traffic ceased on 14th May 1964. (Stations UK)

Top 51. Seen on 3rd February 1966 is the up side, devoid of its canopy. Passenger service was withdrawn eleven days later. The footbridge had six flights of steps - see map. (D.K.Jones)

Lower 52. Speeding through on 7th August 1983 is no. 47451 with the 15.05 Euston to Holyhead express. The roadway leads to the old wharf and has user-worked gates, usually padlocked. (D.H.Mitchell)

HOLYWELL JUNCTION

Football
Ground

S. Ps

M.P.

S. B

S.Ps

L.B

Bodlondeb

Plâs-yn-morfa

Swan & Station
Inn

Ty-gwyn

Capel Ebenezer
(Independent)

P.H.

P.H.   P.H.

Flagstaff

Stone P.H.
Royal
Hotel

P.H.

Club

Chy.

Smithy

Holy Trinity
Church

Post
Office

St. Weir

Abbey Mills
(Paper)

F.P.

XIV.   The 1911 edition has the embankments of the Holywell
Mineral Railway north-south on the right page. Completed in
1860, it crossed the C&HR on the level until 1867, when the
bridge shown was built. The LNWR relaid the branch and opened
it to passengers on 1st July 1912. The goods yard was completely
relaid to allow a curve to be provided to a bay platform. The
siding top left was for long used by the engineers.

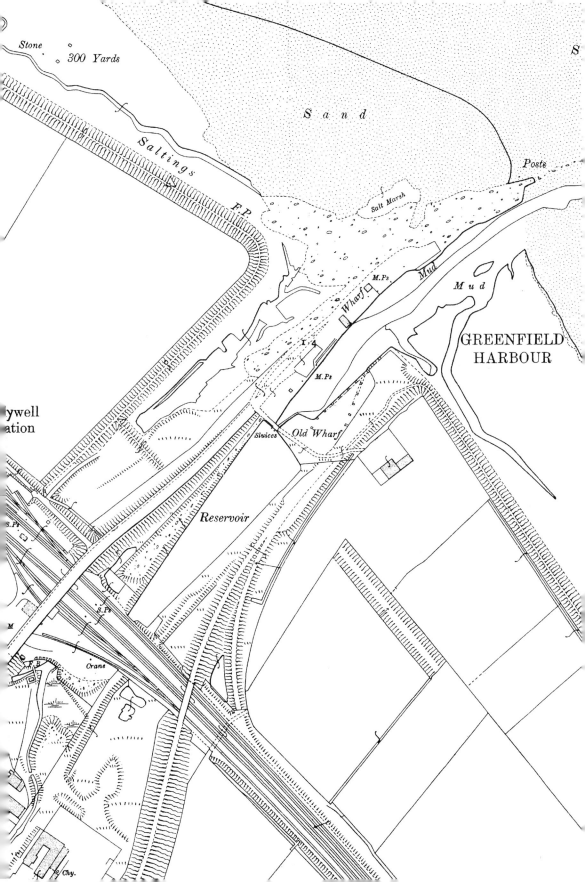

Stone

300 Yards

S

S a n d

Saltings

Posts

F.P.

Salt Marsh

Wharf

Mud

M.Ps

Mud

GREENFIELD
HARBOUR

M.Ps

ywell
ation

Old Wharf

Sluices

Reservoir

S.P.

S.P.

M

Crane

F.B

Chy.

53.   The station received its suffix when the branch opened. The bay is seen soon after its opening, when the seats still show the old name. No. 2518 is an LNWR 2-4-2T. (Lens of Sutton coll.)

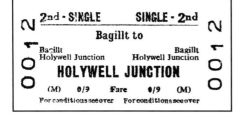

2nd - SINGLE   SINGLE - 2nd

Bagillt to

Bagillt   Bagillt
Holywell Junction   Holywell Junction

HOLYWELL JUNCTION

(M)   0/9   Fare   0/9   (M)

For conditions see over   For conditions see over

0012   0012

British Rlys (M)   British Rlys (M)
MONTHLY RET   FOR CONDITIONS
Valid One Month   SEE BACK

THIRD CLASS   MONTHLY RET
                                        Valid One Month

Holywell Town   Holywell Junc

TO   TO

HOLYWELL JUNC.   HOLYWELL TOWN

RB For conditions   Third
      see back   Class   RB

Fare -/6½ Z   Fare -/6½ Z

4345   4345

54.   This westward panorama of the coastal plain is from the road bridge to the wharf in about 1935. The goods yard was in two parts; this section included the cattle dock. (Stations UK)

55.   On the down fast line on 10th August 1953 is 4-6-0 no. 44738 with the 4.30pm Manchester to Llandudno service. The line to the bay is on the right. (H.C.Casserley)

56.   The push-pull train to Holywell Town is standing in the bay on 4th September 1954, its penultimate day of operation. The wooden platform is over an area of marshland. (Colour-Rail.com)

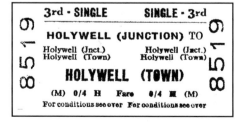

CHESTER & HOLYHEAD RAILWAY TABLE of TOLLS AUTHORISED TO BE TAKEN.	
1st Class Passengers	3 d. Per Mile
2nd Class Passengers	2½ d.
3rd Class Passengers	1½ d.
Horse, Mule or Ass	6 d.
Ox, Cow, Bull or Neat Cattle	3 d.
Calf or Pig	1½ d.
Sheep, Lamb or other small Animal	1 d.
Four-Wheel Carriage	6 d.
Two-Wheel Carriage	4 d.
Coal, Stones, Clay, Sand, Dung, Lime and Limestone and all undressed Materials for the Repair of Public Roads or Highways conveyed any distance not exceeding 15 Miles	2d. Per Ton Per Mile
Conveyed exceeding 15 Miles	1½ d.

57.   The fare table was recorded on the same day. It was situated on the platform wall of the booking office and was just over a century out of date. (Colour-Rail.com)

58.   Closure to passengers came on 14th February 1966, days after this photograph was taken. This was one of the original C&HR stations and survives with a Grade II listing. (D.K.Jones coll.)

59.　　No. 47324 runs east with a spoil train on 8th August 1982. The 1903 signal box appears here and in picture 56. Its 54-lever frame was still in use in 2011 and the track layout was unchanged. (D.H.Mitchell)

60.　　A year later and we look from the other side of the bridge at Courtaulds' Greenfield plant and no. 47459 with the 14.36 Manchester Victoria to Llandudno. To the right of it is a little used extension of the down goods loop. (D.H.Mitchell)

WEST OF HOLYWELL

61.   Apparently resting in the fields is the 4800-ton *Duke of Lancaster*. It is seen on 16th August 1988 in the company of no. 47453, which is working the 09.50 Euston to Holyhead. The ship was built by Harland & Wolff in 1956 in Belfast for the BR Belfast-Heysham ferry service. (H.Ballantyne)

62.   The vessel was sold in 1979 and became "a fun ship", which was not a success. It was subsequently used for storing fashion merchandise and is seen in September 1979. By 2011, it was a rusting eyesore and seemed to be sitting in an open grave. (C.L.Caddy)

MOSTYN

XV. The 1910 issue includes the important iron works, which also produced large amounts of manganese during the Russo-Japanese war of 1904-10 and World War I, the ore coming from local mines.

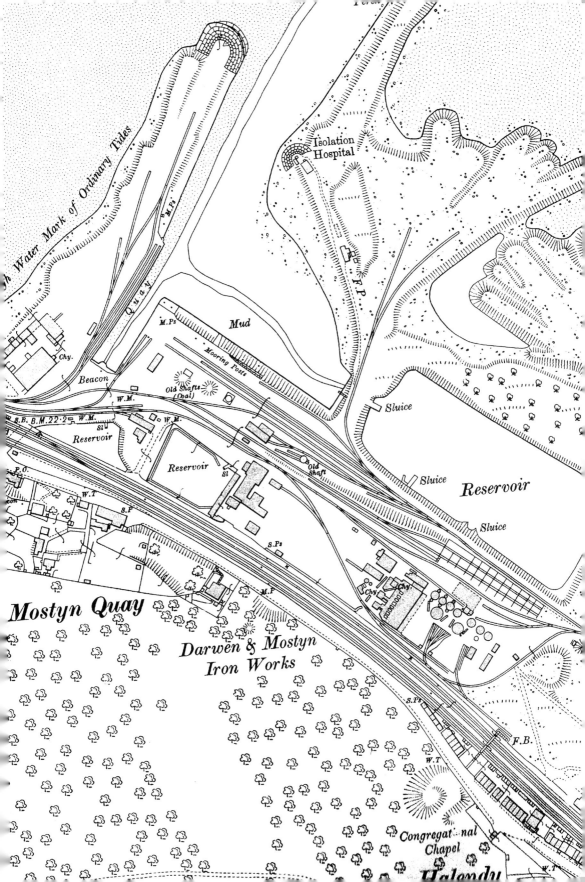

High Water Mark of Ordinary Tides

Quay

Isolation
Hospital

F.P

Chy.

Beacon

M.Ps

Mud

Mooring Posts

Old Shafts
(Coal)

W.M.

Sluice

S.B. B.M. 22·2

W.M.

Sl.

W.M.

Reservoir

Reservoir

Sl.

Old
Shaft

Sluice

Reservoir

P.O.

W.T

S.P

Sluice

S.Ps

M.P

S.P

Chy.

Chy.

Mostyn Quay

*Darwen & Mostyn
Iron Works*

S.Ps

W.T

F.B.

W.T

*Congregat nal
Chapel*

Halcndy

63.   A new footbridge came in 1897 and received roofing in 1904. Quadrupling was completed on 22nd June 1902, but few trains called at the island platform. (Stations UK)

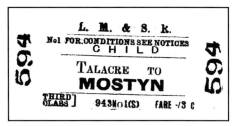

64.   A hipped-roof shelter was built on the up side in 1884 and this similar one came after the quadrupling. This 1961 view reveals the loss of the footbridge roof and the island platform shelter. (D.K.Jones)

65.   An eastward panorama on 3rd February 1966 includes the works built for iron production, together with the goods yard, which had closed on 4th May 1964. Nearby was Bychton Colliery from 1859. (D.K.Jones)

66.   The north elevation was recorded on the same day, together with two armourial panels. Passenger service ceased on 14th February 1966. (D.K.Jones coll.)

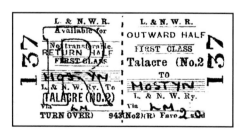

67.   Seen on 8th August 1982 is no. 47482 with the 14.08 Holyhead to Euston. Sidings are evident on the right and the small signals control others. (D.H.Mitchell)

68.   Two signal boxes were provided in 1902, but the one west of the station was short lived, but is on the map. The one seen was fitted with 40 levers and was still in use in 2011 and the dock sidings were still connected. No. 47482 is heading the 15.00 from Euston to Holyhead on 8th August 1982. (D.H.Mitchell)

TALACRE

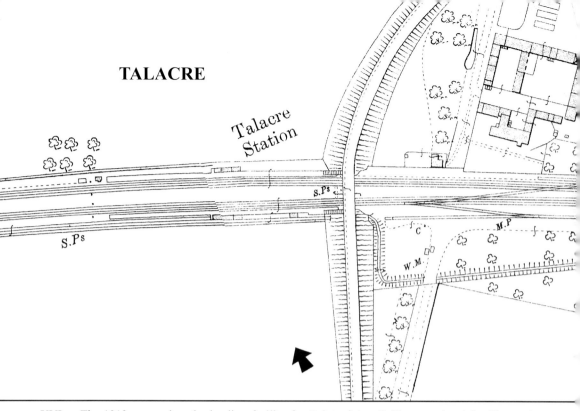

XVI.   The 1912 survey has the loading facility for Point of Ayr Colliery on the right. The station opened on 1st May 1903, following the quadrupling of the area. The road bridge was also new then; the southern part of the old road was used for access to the goods yard. The two cranes are marked C.

69.   The first of two westward views has the details of the down platform and both emphasise the great width of the coastal plain in this vicinity. (R.M.Casserley coll.)

➜ 70. The up platform had similar facilities and both were illuminated by paraffin lamps. The background is now blanketed by caravans. The station closed to goods on 4th May 1964 and to passengers on 14th February 1966. (Lens of Sutton coll.)

lawndy

F.P.

W.M.

Screen
(Coal)

Incline

C

S.Ps

L. & N.W.R.
CHESTER & HOLYHE

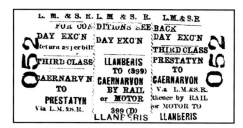

← 71. Point of Ayr Colliery (left) was productive from 1883 until 1996, much of the output going by sea. In 1953, 738 men raised 213,000 tons of coal. The wagons are on one of the two long parallel sidings, which formed a loop. No. 40192 speeds west while hauling the 14.36 Manchester Victoria to Llandudno on 8th August 1982. (D.H.Mitchell)

72. From the other side of the bridge on the same day, we see no. 47525 running close to the long shunting neck. It was controlled by the 24-lever Talacre signal box, which was still in use in 2011. The next box west was Nant Hall, which had only five levers. That box served as a block post for the down lines only. It was in intermittent use from 1936 to 1975. (D.H.Mitchell)

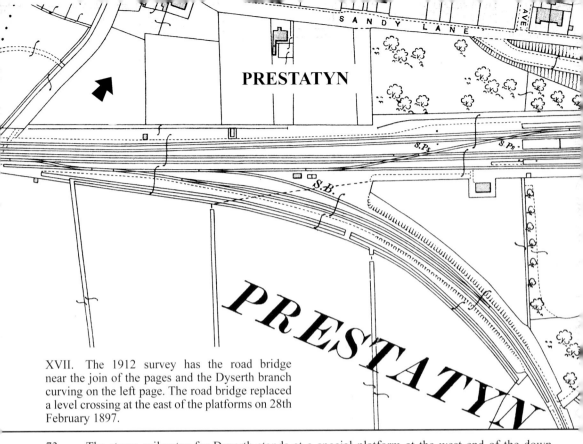

PRESTATYN

PRESTATYN

XVII. The 1912 survey has the road bridge near the join of the pages and the Dyserth branch curving on the left page. The road bridge replaced a level crossing at the east of the platforms on 28th February 1897.

73.   The steam railmotor for Dyserth stands at a special platform at the west end of the down platform. All trains for Dyserth had to run across the left page and then reverse onto the branch, thus a driving compartment at each end was an advantage. (J.Langford coll.)

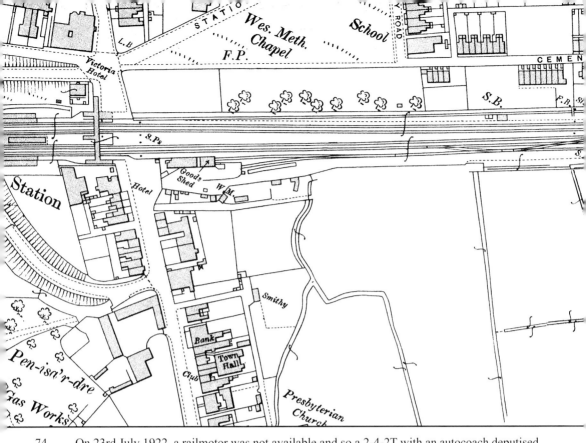

74.   On 23rd July 1922, a railmotor was not available and so a 2-4-2T with an autocoach deputised. The inward angled steps would be inclined outwards at halts with ground level platforms. The platforms here had been greatly lengthened in 1920-21. (Bentley coll.)

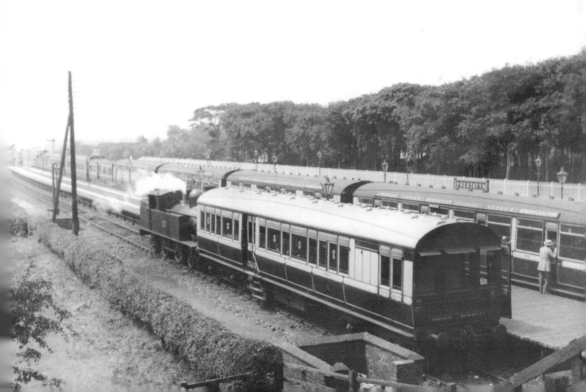

75. This is the first station on our journey to attract holidaymakers in large numbers and here is a card which would have been posted home bearing the words "we have arrived safely". Few had telephones in the six-wheeled coach era.
(Lens of
Sutton coll.)

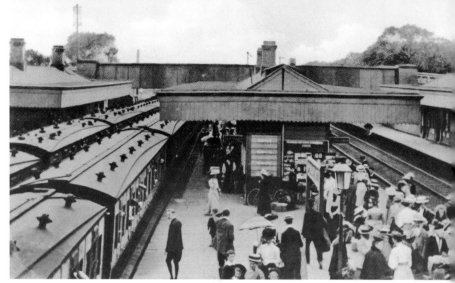

76. After one successful Summer, the nearby holiday camp was taken over by the Army. Locals look on as the military move in. The bridge roof would not last much longer.
(A.Dudman coll.)

77. An eastward panorama has the site of the level crossing at the end of the platforms. The first station had been beyond it and part of its buildings are evident. The population grew from 1261 in 1901 to 11,490 in 1961. The island platform came into use when the quadruple track was completed on 2nd June 1901.
(Lens of
Sutton coll.)

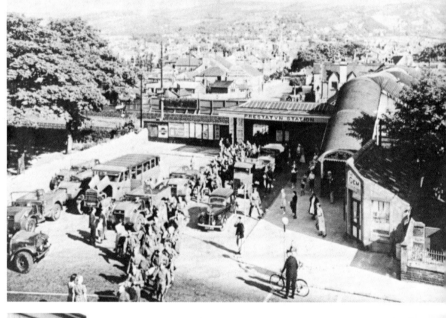

78. A closer look at the old station is to be had as "Black 5" 4-6-0 no. 45275 approaches with the 9.30am Manchester Exchange to Llandudno on 18th August 1962. The connection to the goods yard can be seen; it closed on 4th May 1964. (E.Wilmshurst)

79. No. 45275 adds to the unwelcome environment on 25th June 1966. Staff and visitors suffer the rain and it was a long walk to a bus or taxi. The main sign mentions Prestatyn Holiday Camp, which was much further. The footbridge was erected in 1899. (H.C.Casserley)

80. Pulling in on 23rd August 1975 is no. 47438 with the 09.48 Rhyl to Crewe. The wagons on the left are on the former Dyserth branch, while those in the centre are on its bay line. (T.Heavyside)

81. Seen from the footbridge on the same day is a train bound for Manchester Victoria. It is formed of the 08.32 from Bangor and the 08.45 from Llandudno which joined at Llandudno Junction. The building was prefabricated in sections in Crewe Works in 1879 and was fully restored in 1979. (T.Heavyside)

82. No. 47019 arrives with the 09.30 Llandudno to Scarborough on 6th August 1983. Water troughs had been laid in the distance in 1885. The 30-lever signal box opened in March 1907 and was still in use in 2011, but with 45 levers. Further west was Rhyl Sands box from 1913 to 1967, with 15 levers. Platform 1 (left) was usable into the 1990s. (D.H.Mitchell)

83. Two photographs from July 1996 record the original buildings, by then listed structures. We have glimpsed these in picture 78. The goods shed housed a 30-cwt crane. (D.G.Smith)

84. The view from the south reveals that brick was used for the main building and stone for the goods shed. This arrived at least ten years after the line opened. There was a second signal box nearby from 1901 to 1931. (D.G.Smith)

85. The 1987 footbridge was demolished on 20th March 2010, to meet fresh legislation. A temporary one was in use on 29th December 2010 as the 07.29 Birmingham International to Holyhead called. The eastern half of the platform was out of use and so no. 158827 waits away from the canopies. (L.Davies)

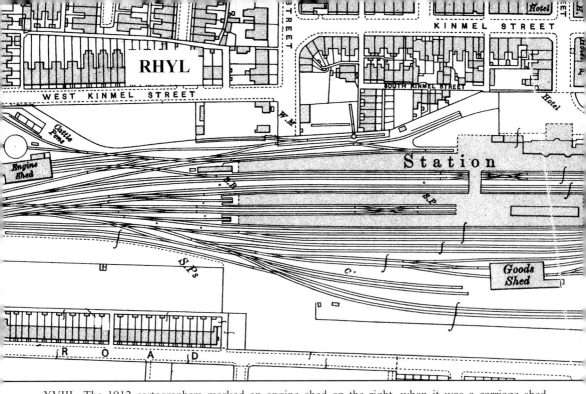

XVIII. The 1912 cartographers marked an engine shed on the right, when it was a carriage shed, completed in about 1900. The engine shed is on the left and the 50ft turntable shown was increased to 60ft in 1938, by removing the cattle dock.

86. A westward panorama from the road bridge in about 1920 features the down platform and its unusual glazed screen parallel to the coaches. This was to improve weather protection for passengers and was replicated at Llandudno Junction. (Stations UK)

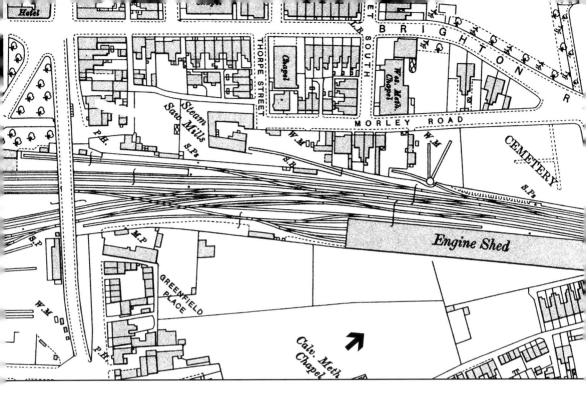

87.	The up platform was well protected and furnished, the main entrance being that side. Enlargement and rebuilding began in 1878. On the left is a train for the Vale of Clwyd line to Denbigh, a service which lasted until 1955. (Lens of Sutton coll.)

88.   An up ex-
press is on one of
the two through
lines on 9th July
1960, as crowds
wait for the next
stopping train. The
many chimneys re-
quired substantial
labour to keep the
fires burning.
(Bentley coll.)

89.   The three-
road engine shed
was often crowded;
there were 27 loco-
motives based here
in 1950 and 14 in
1959. The photo-
graph is from 8th
June 1960 and the
turntable is in front
of the water tank on
the right.
(Colour-Rail.com)

90.   The turn-
table is in the fore-
ground in this view
from May 1961.
The first one was
provided in 1849,
but it was nearer
to the station. The
shed code was 7D in
1948-52 and 6K un-
til closure in 1963.
(R.S.Carpenter)

91. This August 1964 eastward view reveals the great width of the footbridge. Traffic grew enormously, at a greater rate than the population. This rose from 8473 in 1901 to 21,440 in 1961. The road bridge in the background replaced a level crossing in 1878. (H.C.Casserley)

92. Class 5 4-6-0 no. 44771 was shunting the goods yard on 10th October 1966 and would leave for Denbigh at 12.45. The route would close in 1968. The yard was in use until June 1984; it had a 5-ton crane. (D.Johnson)

93.   We are at the west end of the station on 9th June 1973 and witness no. 330 passing with a Freightliner bound for Holyhead, a regular service at that time. The bays had lost their track and the goods yard was mainly used for carriage storage. (T.Heavyside)

94.   There were private sidings listed east of the station in 1938 for R.Evans & Co., Roberts, and Rhyl UDC. We look east from the main road on 4th August 1979. The carriage shed no longer served its original purpose, but No. 1 Box did. Its 90-lever frame came into use on 27th May 1900 and it was still functioning in 2011. (T.Heavyside)

95.   No. 2 Box is seen on 8th August 1989 as 4-6-0 no. 5407 passes with "The North Wales Coast Express", a special from Crewe to Holyhead. The two bay platforms had been on the right. (T.Heavyside)

96.   In the Summer of 1938, over 100,000 tickets were collected each month. No wonder wide platforms were needed. There is little sign of activity on 20th December 1987. There had earlier been a substantial porte-cochère here. (C.L.Caddy)

97.　　This is the same view as in picture 94, but on 21st August 1990. Sidings for the engineers have arrived and the loop line has gone, as has the up main line. The down one was still in use in 2011. No. 31420 approaches with the 09.44 Manchester Victoria to Llandudno. (T.Heavyside)

98.　　No. 2 Box was also built in 1900, but it had 126 levers. Closure came on 25th March 1990, but a Grade II listing was applied. A class 43 HST in InterCity livery accelerates away, while working from Euston to Holyhead, sometime in 1996. (Colour-Rail.com)

2. Holywell Town Branch

XIX.   The 1949 edition at 6ins to 1 mile shows the full length of the branch and the proximity of the terminus to the town centre.

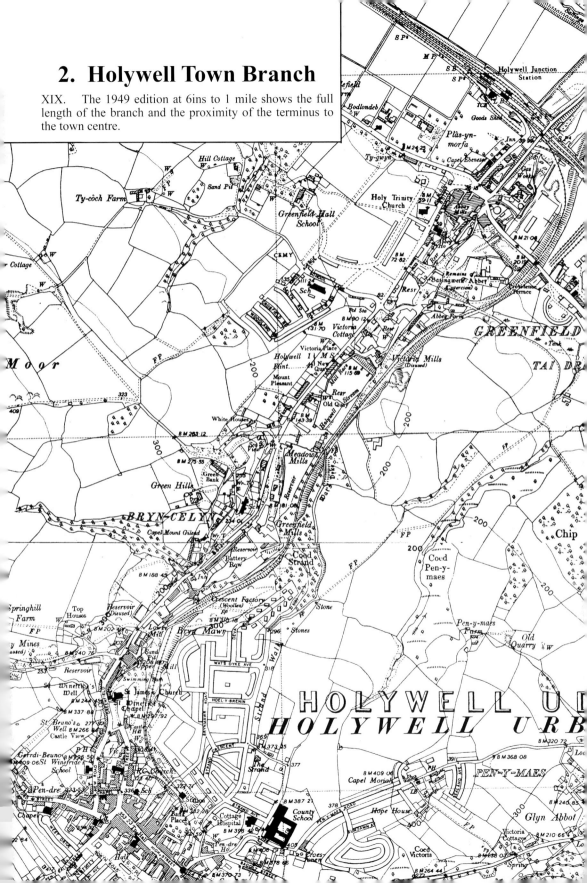

99.   The main line is in the background as "Coal Tank" no. 27585 propels its coach round the initial curve towards the "catch point". The severe gradient on the 1½ mile branch averaged 1 in 27. The straight track was termed the "safety siding" and the point was worked by the fireman. This track was on the original route to the docks. (W.A.Camwell/SLS coll.)

ST. WINEFRIDE'S HALT

100.   St. Winefride's Chapel and Well are lower left on the map, but the nearby halt is not, although it opened and closed with the line. Crescent siding (right) remained open until 11th August 1957. (Lens of Sutton coll.)

101.   The word HALT did not appear to be used until 1939, but the spelling of the name always differed from that used more widely. The three views are from early postcards. (Stations UK)

102.   A northward panorama includes some of the many mill ponds, with the sea in the distance. The woollen industry was important in this valley for many generations. (Lens of Sutton coll.)

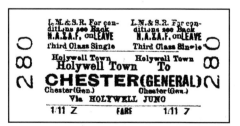

HOLYWELL TOWN

103.   We have a further two postcards, this one including an LNWR 2-4-2T, a type used regularly until 1950. (Lens of Sutton coll.)

104.   The bunting suggests that this and the previous view were recorded on opening day. Few passenger lines were so steep as to have a vertical bend in the platform, unless underground.
(Lens of Sutton coll.)

105.   The end of the line is in sight, the ground rising steeply beyond it. Class 2F 0-6-2T no. 27585 is seen in about 1948, together with the sole "Hawks Eye" sign. (W.A.Camwell/SLS coll.)

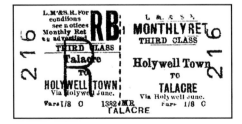

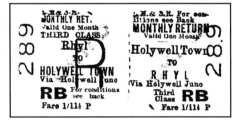

106.   The driving compartment includes the later shades in this post-1950 view of the approach to the goods yard. The Ivatt class 2MT 2-6-2T type was introduced to the branch in January 1950. (N.R.Knight/SLS coll.)

107.   Locomotives had a stiff climb on the branch and passengers had likewise upon arrival. The town housed 7139 souls in 1901 and 8470 in 1961, but traffic fell as bus transport improved. (R.S.Carpenter coll.)

108.   Freight trains were limited to five wagons and had to include two brake vans, the locomotive being at the downhill end. The crane is evident; it could lift five tons. (R.S.Carpenter coll.)

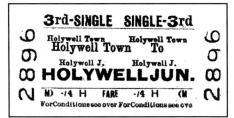

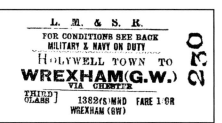

109. It was only the driver who had to change ends after arrival, but all gather round for the rare visit of a photographer in 1953. On the left is the stretcher cupboard, a standard feature soon to disappear from all stations. (H.C.Casserley)

110. The last day of operation was 4th September 1954 and performing on that sad occasion was 2-6-2T no. 41276. (Colour-Rail.com)

3. Dyserth Branch

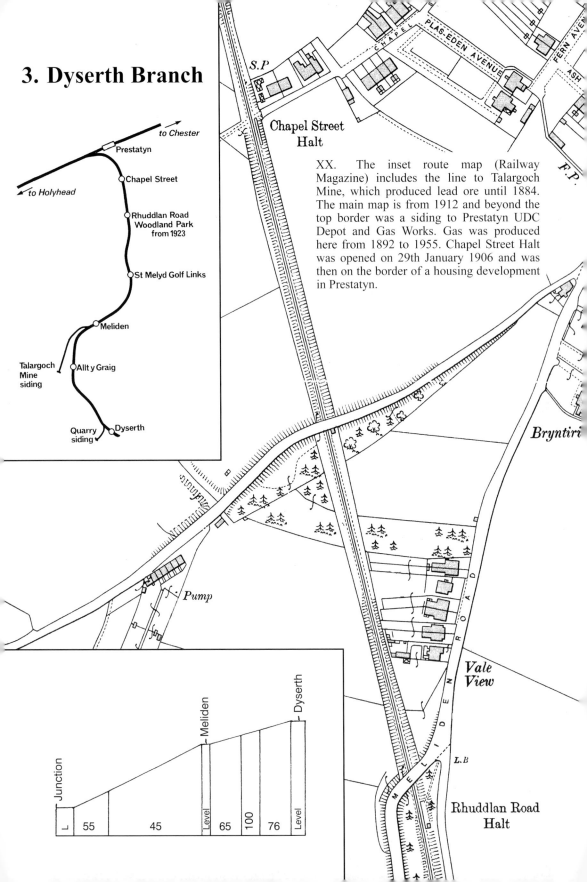

to Chester

Prestatyn

to Holyhead

Chapel Street

Rhuddlan Road
Woodland Park
from 1923

St Melyd Golf Links

Meliden

Talargoch
Mine
siding

Allt y Graig

Quarry
siding

Dyserth

S.P

Chapel Street
Halt

XX. The inset route map (Railway Magazine) includes the line to Talargoch Mine, which produced lead ore until 1884. The main map is from 1912 and beyond the top border was a siding to Prestatyn UDC Depot and Gas Works. Gas was produced here from 1892 to 1955. Chapel Street Halt was opened on 29th January 1906 and was then on the border of a housing development in Prestatyn.

Bryntiri

Pump

Vale
View

L.B

Junction

Meliden

Dyserth

L	55	45	Level	65	100	76	Level

Rhuddlan Road
Halt

WOODLAND PARK HALT

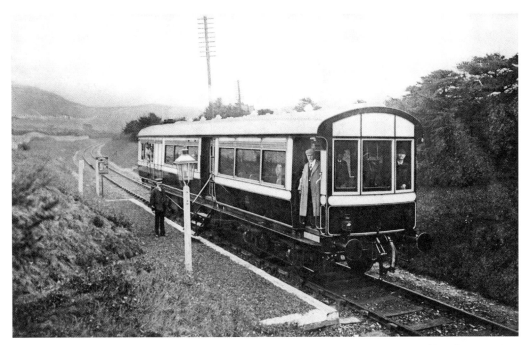

111.   This stop opened with the branch and was called Rhuddlan Road Halt until 11th May 1923. This was the first LNWR branch to be operated by railmotors and they ran here until World War I. (P.Q.Treloar coll.)

112.   A small hut arrived after a few years and the railmotors lost their light end panels. The 36 telephone wires were "National"; the branch had none. South of here, St. Melyd Golf Links Halt was opened on 1st October 1923. (Lens of Sutton coll.)

MELIDEN

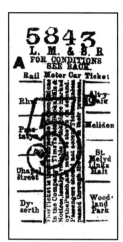

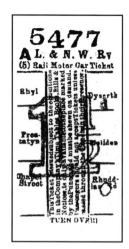

XXI.   The siding on the left of this 1916 map had earlier been extended to Talargoch Mine and was removed in 1918. The siding serving the quarry was added in 1899 and lasted until 1918. Further south was a siding for the quarry at Dyserth Castle from 1903 until 1931. The limestone went to Mostyn mainly. The village housed 478 souls in 1901.

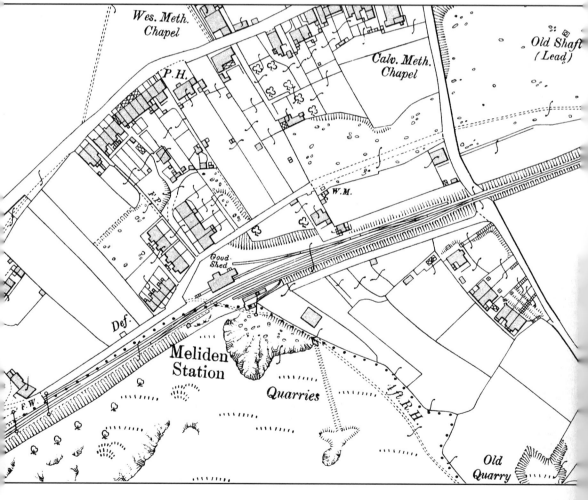

113.   On the left is the quarry siding and a railmotor is on the line to Dyserth. A halt was added on this section of the branch at Allt-y-Craig on 1st February 1929, although it had only one "l" initially. (Lens of Sutton coll.)

114.   The quarry siding had once passed between the running line and the goods shed, which is seen on 18th July 1963. Public freight traffic ceased here on 1st April 1957, parcels having been discontinued on 1st December 1951. (R.M.Casserley)

DYSERTH

XXII.   The station building is the tiny hut to the right of the word "Station" on this 1913 edition. A local landowner undertook earthworks to extend the line east to Marian Mill, but track was never laid. The siding curving to the quarry (left) was opened on 25th February 1885. A cattle pen was added in 1923. Lower left, a narrow gauge railway passes over Newmarket Road on a bridge.

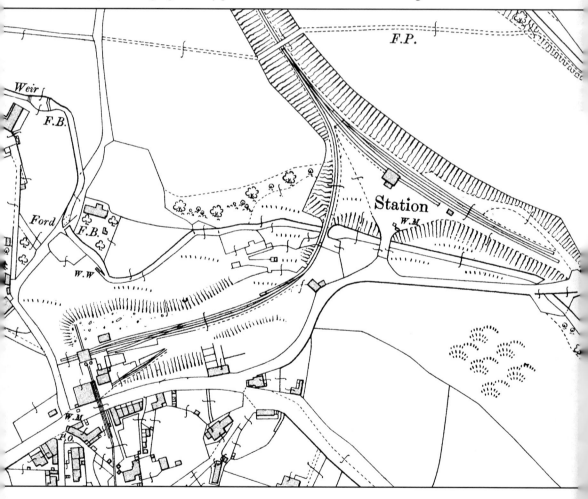

115.　　A railmotor stands on the approach to the station, with the quarry siding on the left. The expensive bridge carried only a footpath and farm animals. To the left of the camera was a bridge over a stream, across which locomotives were not allowed to pass. (Lens of Sutton coll.)

116.　　This panorama towards Prestatyn has the tiny building once used by passengers on the left; next is the goods shed and on the right is the 1909 store of the Vale of Clwyd Farmers Ltd. General goods traffic ceased on 4th May 1964. Rabbits and mushrooms had been in some of the parcels despatched. There was a camping coach here in Summers of the mid-1920s. Station staffing ceased in 1951 and thus so did parcel traffic. (Lens of Sutton coll.)

117.   Few people travelled on the branch after 1930 until the RCTS ran a railtour on 2nd October 1955 and 2-6-4T no. 42461 propelled three coaches up the hill. The Wirral Railway Circle took two 3-car DMUs up the branch on 22nd March 1969 and the LCGB made a visit on 11th October 1969. (T.J.Edgington)

118.   The former station building was recorded on 18th July 1963. Tickets had been issued through a hatch between the doors on the front. The village population had been only 745 in 1901, when campaigning for a passenger service began. However, almost 30,000 journeys were made in 1906, mainly by holidaymakers. (R.M.Casserley)

119.   Class 2 diesels were used in the final years and no. D5140 was in charge on 11th May 1967, a very misty day. There was a 30-cwt crane inside the goods shed. (J.M.Tolson/F.Hornby)

120.   Limestone was sent for use as a flux to the steelworks at Shotton and Mostyn Ironworks. Lime was also produced on site and stone was conveyed from the crushing plant (left) to the kilns in 2ft 7ins gauge wagons. Ageing production equipment and a declining steel industry meant that the branch closed on 7th September 1973 and the quarry followed in 1981. (Tilcon Ltd.)

MP Middleton Press

EVOLVING THE ULTIMATE RAIL ENCYCLOPEDIA

Easebourne Lane, Midhurst, West Sussex.
GU29 9AZ   Tel:01730 813169

www.middletonpress.co.uk   email:info@middletonpress.co.uk
A-978 0 906520 B- 978 1 873793 C- 978 1 901706 D-978 1 904474 E - 978 1 906008

All titles listed below were in print at time of publication - please check current availability by looking at our website - **www.middletonpress.co.uk** or by requesting a Brochure which includes our *LATEST* RAILWAY TITLES also our TRAMWAY, TROLLEYBUS, MILITARY and WATERWAYS series